MW01124952

More of God's Promises Kept

Devotions for Children
inspired by
Charles Spurgeon

Catherine Mackenzie

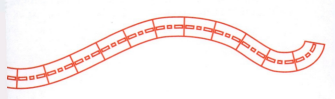

10 9 8 7 6 5 4 3 2 1

Copyright © 2021 Catherine Mackenzie
Paperback ISBN: 978-1-5271-0619-2

Published by Christian Focus Publications,
Geanies House, Fearn, Tain, Ross-shire,
IV20 1TW, Scotland, U.K.
www.christianfocus.com
email: info@christianfocus.com

Cover design by Pete Barnsley
Printed and bound in Turkey

Scripture quotations are from the King James Version
and the author's own paraphrase.

Who was Charles Spurgeon?

Charles Haddon Spurgeon was a Baptist preacher. He was born in the United Kingdom in 1834 and by the time of his death in 1892 he was known as the "Prince of Preachers". Spurgeon was pastor of the congregation of the New Park Street Chapel and then of the Metropolitan Tabernacle in London for thirty-eight years. As well as preaching many sermons he also wrote a great many books, and hymns. Many Christians, even today, love the daily devotional book he wrote: *The Chequebook of the Bank of Faith*. This book has been based on the topics and Scriptures he used. In a culture where few use a chequebook this publication needed more than a simple rewrite. However, these little devotions have been inspired by what Spurgeon wrote. Hopefully this reimagining of some of his devotions will help a new generation to appreciate his teaching but, most importantly, the Word of God. When you see some words in the text written in red these are taken almost directly from Spurgeon's own writings. The rest are either explaining or representing what he wrote.

Catherine Mackenzie

Contents

1. Silly Sheep

Chequebook Date: 19 April
Bible Verse: For thus saith the Lord GOD, Behold, I, even I, will both search for sheep, and seek them out (Ezekiel 34:11).

Are sheep really silly?

I have often heard people describe sheep as stupid animals, but I'm not sure if that is really what they are. I think perhaps they are mostly stubborn. And when you are stubborn you are also probably a bit foolish too.

I've seen some sheep do their best to get out of their fields because they think that the grass on the other side of the fence looks juicier, greener, tastier. So they clamber through a gap, or they jump over the fence, taking no heed to the fact that once they've escaped the field, they are putting

8

themselves in the path of danger. There are often fast cars on the road outside the field, and there might even be wild animals or dogs that would hurt them.

So, yes, sometimes sheep are silly because they want their own way.

That's one of the reasons sheep need shepherds. A shepherd looks out for them, by making sure they are safe.

The Bible often tells us that human beings are very like sheep – we are stubborn and a bit silly too. God has to look after us as a shepherd looks after the sheep. Human beings – men, women and children – often want to lead their lives their own way. They don't want God making the decisions even though his decisions are best.

Some people seem to think that sin is fun, something to be enjoyed, but sin is something that destroys us and poisons our life. It is to be avoided at all costs. But sinners who do not trust God are like foolish sheep, who think that the green grass on the dangerous cliff top is the best grass to eat. The shepherd needs to grab those sheep and take them back to the field immediately.

Jesus is a great seeking shepherd as well as a saving shepherd. Jesus seeks and finds sinners – the ones that don't know him. Jesus finds those people who know nothing about him or his Word.

Then Jesus saves his sheep. A good shepherd looks out for his flock and takes them away from danger – sometimes putting himself in harm's way. Jesus saves sinners who are like wandering sheep. He not only put himself in danger in order to save us – he died instead of us.

God has never lost a single one of his sheep. They are always found. They are always safe. They may have fallen into sin and great suffering, yet God will never let one of them go so far away from God that they can't be saved. In fact, it is impossible for any of the Lord's people to do that. However hard someone tries to run away from God, God will chase them harder. However far away someone tries to get from God, God will keep pursuing them. Jesus will not lose one of those that God the Father has given to him.

What you can do: It is a point of honour with Jesus to seek and to save all the flock, without a single exception. Keep praying for those you know who are lost. We have a good hope for those that God has made us love. This hope is so great that we will always want to pray for them. We know that God will find them.

Pray: Dear Heavenly Father, I am like a lost sheep. I have wandered away from you. You have said you will seek and save every one of your sheep. Please forgive my sins. In the name of Jesus. Amen.

2. Favourite Things

Chequebook Date: 28 April
Bible Verse: I will dwell in them, and walk in them; and I will be their God, and they shall be my people (2 Corinthians 6:16).

What is your most treasured possession?

Is it your bike? A favourite toy? Perhaps if you are older you own some jewellery — so it might be a ring or a necklace that you treasure. Maybe it's your money bank or wallet? It might be a mobile phone.

I have several favourite things: a necklace my parents gave me, a Bible I got from my granny, a box of letters and keepsakes I've received from friends and family over the years. Sometimes favourite things can be valuable because they are expensive, but sometimes they are treasured for other reasons.

Even though necklaces or letters from loved ones are precious belongings that is all they are – they are only belongings. These items themselves don't own anything. They are owned by you and that's it.

If you added people to your list of cherished possessions, it would be different. Parents and siblings belong to you as they are family. You also belong to them. But people are not like possessions. They have life in them and are to be treated differently to the way you would treat a bike or a phone.

As a human being you also belong to someone else – not just your family and friends. You, as a human being, always belong to God because he has made you. He is your Creator. If you have trusted in Jesus Christ to save you from sin then he is also your Saviour. He made you, but he has also saved you. Christ died for the ungodly and it is only through him that your sins can be forgiven.

When you trust in God, you and God are family. You belong to him. He belongs to you.

God will always think of his own people, and they will always think of him. And now that God has saved you and turned you away from sin, your thoughts will always go running after him. When you wake in the morning you will wonder, 'What can I do for God today?' We should always make it our first priority to think about God and do our best for him. And we need to do more than just think about it. We should do it. Thoughts need to become actions. Do what God says.

The good things that we do for God are good in lots of ways, but they don't save us. Jesus is the only one who saves. His sacrifice was the one perfect work that saves sinners. Our good actions are given to us to do by God and through them we glorify God. Glorifying God is exactly what God designed us to do. Glorifying God is when our words and actions show everyone how wonderful God is, and how lovely and loving Jesus is. These good actions are healthy for our souls. It is our chief purpose in life to enjoy and glorify God. Living like this is good. Living for ourselves alone is not good!

So, we belong to God and God belongs to us. God thinks on us and we think about God. God also lives in us and we live in him. Throughout our day, wherever we are, the one true living God walks with us. There is no time or place where he is not with us and we are not with him. What a happy place to be.

 What you should do: Trust God and serve him. Obey him.

Prayer: Dear God, may I trust you and glorify you with my life. This is what you deserve. Lord help me for Jesus' sake. Amen.

3. Pay back Time

Chequebook Date: 29 April
Bible Verse: Say not thou, I will recompense evil;
but wait on the Lord and he shall save thee
(Proverbs 20:22).

Have you ever fallen out with someone and been told to 'Cool down'?

Often when two people disagree things get worse rather than better. Each person wants their own way and in order to get it they will squabble, then argue, then fall out, then fight.

The Lord Jesus Christ set us the best example of forgiving when he died on the cross. He had been so badly treated – whipped and beaten and nailed to a cross – yet in the middle of it all, Jesus prayed for those who had hurt him, 'Father forgive them for they know not what they are doing' (Luke 23:34).

When we find ourselves hurt, either physically or emotionally, it is good to forgive rather than to think nasty thoughts about how to get our own back. 'But that makes me out to be a big loser,' you say. 'Shouldn't I stick up for myself and put those people in their place?'

Is that what Jesus would have you do? Today's Bible verse says, 'Wait on the Lord and he shall save.' Just be calm and quiet. Wait on God – tell him all about it.

In the Bible we read that King Hezekiah received a frightening letter from his enemy, the King of Assyria. This man was evil and proud. He arrogantly wrote to Hezekiah about how God was not going to save the people of Israel.

Hezekiah took his concerns to the Lord. And God replied, 'I will defend this city, to save it, for my own sake, and for my servant David's sake.'

So, what happened? Well, that night the angel of the Lord struck the camp of the Assyrians so that 185,000 soldiers were wiped out. The King of Assyria's army was utterly defeated without a single Israelite soldier even breaking a sweat.

So, what does this story teach us? We can trust in God. As God delivered Hezekiah he will find a way to rescue you out of your troubles. God will find a way of deliverance for you. How he will do it neither you nor I can guess, but do it he will. When God saves you from your enemy, that is a far better result than you dealing out your own pay back.

What you should do: Don't be angry. Leave your request for justice with the Judge of the whole world.

Prayer: Lord God and loving Heavenly Father, may my spirit be one of gentleness and forgiveness. Forgive me for my sin and forgetfulness. Amen.

4. Sowing and Waiting

Chequebook Date: 2 May
Bible Verse: He that soweth to the Spirit shall
of the Spirit reap life everlasting
(Galatians 6:8).

'What are they doing?'

That's what a dog or a cat might think if they saw you digging in the garden. The dog might wonder why human beings are burying tiny little things in the soil, never to dig them up again. 'I do a much better job of burying my bones,' he might think.

The cat may say to herself, 'Those human beings are so silly to scratch around in the dirt with nothing to show for it. Why do they get so dirty. I wouldn't.' Cats, you see, are very good at keeping clean. However, by the time the warmer weather comes along and the

19

cat and the dog have long forgotten about their humans doing silly things in the garden, something has begun to happen. Seeds start to sprout. Eventually a good gardener will have an excellent crop of vegetables or several bouquets of flowers. The hard work pays off.

Now, just as the cat and dog think that gardening is a waste of time, many people who do not trust the Lord God think that being a Christian is foolish. However, God clearly says in Psalm 14:1 that it is the one who doesn't believe in him who is foolish.

A gardener has a lot of work to do. Those who trust in God have to work hard too. Their work doesn't save them – that is God's work. But a Christian must do what they can to obey God and show the world how wonderful God is. This is how God's children are made ready for heaven, that glorious place believers go to when they die.

A gardener has to wait months to see what happens in his soil. A Christian has to wait a lifetime before they finally see what God has done in their soul. Sometimes God's plan is for his children to get to heaven sooner than they might have expected. It is a fact of life that you do not know when you will die, you just know that it will happen one day.

Somewhere in the middle of Africa, one of the largest rivers in the world, the Nile, begins in a muddy puddle. Eventually, it flows to the ocean passing through countries, giving water to millions on the way. People get great help from this river that starts in a puddle.

This life flows on like an ever-deepening, ever-widening river, till it brings us to the ocean of never ending peace, where the life of God is ours for ever. The Christian life has the most amazing end – heaven – when God gives believers the gift of everlasting life, peace, joy, love and God's company.

What you should do: Seek to honour God by obedience to him.

Prayer: Lord, help me to trust in you and obey you. May I spend my life glorifying and enjoying you. Amen.

The Last Promise

Here is the last promise we read in the Bible. It is one that is still to be kept. But because God is faithful, he always does what he says he will do. So, we know that Jesus is going to return one day.

He who testifies to these things says, 'Surely I am coming quickly' (Revelation 22:20).

5. Bugging Bugs

Chequebook Date: 18 May
Bible Verse: And I will restore to you the years
that the locusts hath eaten (Joel 2:25).

What do you think of caterpillars?

They can be so colourful and kind of weird-looking. Sometimes they have strange stripes or spots, sometimes they have little tufts of hair growing out of their backs. They don't really look like the butterflies that they will eventually become. However, in order to become a butterfly they need to eat lots. That's when bugs become bugging. Gardeners fight a continual battle to keep these squirmy creatures under control. Caterpillars munch their way through lots of lettuces, and other leaves and vegetables. Insects that get out of control can do a lot of damage!

Quite often, in the Bible, we hear about an insect that still causes a lot of damage across the world – the locust. It is well-known for gathering in large swarms and eating its way through entire fields of produce. When locusts arrive on a farmer's property, the whole business can lose all its crops in a matter of hours. That's a much bigger problem than just a few caterpillars. Locusts can destroy everything.

In today's Bible verse we hear that, just as a farmer can lose all his produce to a locust swarm, human beings can have their whole lives wasted by sin. God is telling us that sin is just like a ravenous, hungry locust. Sin can eat up the best years of your life. As a young person you have lots of opportunities ahead of you to do good things: learn, love, create and worship God. But sin can tempt anyone of any age to make wrong decisions, so that we waste our time and even destroy our lives as a result. Sometimes the wrong decisions we make bring immediate consequences. We may choose to abuse alcohol and become addicted. We may choose to gamble with our money and have nothing left at the end of it. Sometimes our wrong decisions lead us away from God and his peace. We put our trust in money instead, so that at the end of our lives we die without forgiveness of sins. That is a truly wasted and destroyed life.

However, God is telling you in today's verse that all is not lost. God can turn your life around and lead you on a better path – one that doesn't lead to destruction. Then you can help others. You can show your friends and family that God's way is best. You can help them to make better choices than you did. You can tell them the good news of Jesus Christ, so that they can turn to him and be saved.

Even though sin eats up the good years of a person's life, God can change all that and bring that person back to himself. They can change and their lives can change so that they learn about God, love his Word, and create beautiful praise in worship. The wasted years, by a miracle of love, can be restored. Let us believe it, and live for it, and we may get it.

God can bring you back from sin, but God can also keep you away from sin. Ask the Lord to guide you away from destructive sin, so that your young life brings glory to him.

What you should do: Sometimes God's wonderful promises seem too good to be true. But we should believe them, and live for God and we will experience his truth.

Prayer: Dear Heavenly Father, help me to spend my young years serving you. Save me from throwing away my life on selfish things, and destroying my life with sin. Amen.

6. Sunshine and Sorrows

Chequebook Date: 21 May
Bible Verse: If the clouds be full of rain, they
empty themselves upon the earth
(Ecclesiastes 11:3).

Weather is important.

If there is a wedding planned for the weekend, everyone hopes for sunshine. If you are going to have a barbecue on a summer's afternoon, you want the clouds to stay away. At school, when it's the sports day, if it rains it is sometimes rescheduled for the next week. Running a race when the course is wet and muddy is not pleasant.

So, there are lots of reasons why we hope for good weather. And when we see the skies getting darker, and hear the wind picking up we will feel a bit disappointed if we're planning a garden tea party.

However, in my town there is a slogan carved into one of the pavements which says, 'There is no such thing as bad weather, only unsuitable clothing.' And that is true. If you're outside on a stormy day and you're not wearing boots and a warm jacket, you've only got yourself to blame. You forgot to wear the right clothes. But, even then, it's not too big a deal. The sun will eventually come back. The clouds are only hiding it for a bit.

Also, it's a good thing to realise that the black clouds that are filled with rain can actually be a good thing. The farmer often longs for rain to fall on parched fields. The blacker the clouds, the more likely they are going to give a good fall of water. We wouldn't have rain if we didn't have clouds and without clouds and rain, we wouldn't have green fields. You can't have one without the other.

So, when we see clouds on the horizon and think, 'Oh bother, that's my party ruined,' we should just smile and think, 'Well, at least the garden will get a good drink, and the ducks will be happy.' Ducks like nothing better than splashing about.

Troubles in our lives are a bit like clouds. We sometimes see them coming. We realise that problems are just around the corner – so we worry. But just as we can't have a good fall of rain without clouds, we can't have blessings without troubles. Troubles are dark and bothersome, but they can bring good things with them too. God can bring sorrow to your life, but he does this for a reason. Troubles can teach us to depend on him. Sorrow brings us to love God even more.

God sends us suffering, but he will not always do so. Just as the sun reappears after the rain, God will refresh us with his mercy after times of heartache. God allows us to go through difficult times, but he helps us to get stronger. Then he brings us joy.

Have you ever noticed how there are sweet-smelling flowers after a dark shower? God reminds us that he loves us after we've gone through hard times. Even in the middle of trouble he will remind us that he loves us. There is no limit to how or when God will tell you, 'I love you.'

God's greatest message of love was when his Son, Jesus, died on the cross for the sins of his people. In the middle of his pain and sorrow, he gave the best ever love and blessing, taking the worst ever sorrow and darkness on himself.

 What you should do: Do not worry about the clouds. May flowers are brought to us through the April showers. Our God is near us in the dark! When we look on him, our love makes us glad.

Prayer: Dear God, you are my loving Heavenly Father. My troubles are not troubles to you. When times are hard, help me to see that there will be a future of rejoicing. Amen.

7. Do you run Backwards?

Chequebook Date: 23 May

Bible Verse: For he shall deliver the needy when he crieth; the poor also, and him that hath no helper (Psalm 72:12).

On your marks, get set, go!

If you heard these words would you see someone walking in a zigzag, changing his mind to hop and then do cartwheels? Would you see someone run off and then run back and then look over at the other side of the street and go to get their groceries? Or would you see someone take off quickly, putting one foot after the other, in a straight line, in order to get from the start to the finish as quickly as possible?

I think it's the last one, don't you? That's what you call a race. And it's pretty straightforward. Everybody starts a race at the beginning and ends at the end. It's a simple thing — but important. That's what a race is all about. Some do it very quickly, some people are a lot slower. But they all race forwards — unless they're doing a backwards race which is rather silly.

The most important thing for a runner is to get to the finish. Some people say that life is a bit like a race. Everyone has a beginning to life and everyone has an end. But the most important thing for a sinner like you and me in the race of life is to be saved. When we are saved from sin, it means the end of our life won't be the end but the beginning of our best life ever. However, being saved is something we can't do for ourselves. It's only God who can save. It's only God who can help. So, we need to turn to him.

Why do we need God? We need him to give us food and warmth and water and lots of other things to help our bodies live. But because we are sinners and our sins need forgiveness, we need him to forgive us so that our souls can live forever. That is our greatest need.

Perhaps you think that other things are more important than God. Maybe you think that money, a good education, or a good job are what you need in life. If that's what you are thinking then you are being distracted from the one important thing. What you really need is God. He is your only help in life and death.

Sometimes friends can help us, but that is only because God allows them to. He helps them to help us. So, it's important when we need help to go to the beginning of all help, God. Go straight to God as a runner goes straight to the finish.

Perhaps you feel as though you don't have any friends. But that means that you can go to God to be your friend and your helper. You need help and you need friendship – God is the best helper and the best friend. Without God's saving power you are lost for ever. Cry out to God for help and his salvation, and he will provide all you need. He will rescue you.

You are poor – God is rich. You are helpless – God has all the power you need. You make mistakes – God has never failed.

What you should do: Come to God – he will not refuse you help. Jesus is King – he will not let you perish. Straight-forward makes the best runner: run to the Lord, and not to anything else which is second best.

Prayer: Dear Lord and Heavenly Father, thank you that you are the one and only Saviour. You are the best place that I can go to for help. You have everything I need. Help me to run to you straight away when I have a problem. Amen.

'These words are faithful and true' (Revelation 22:6).

8. Reminding God

Chequebook Date: 28 May
Bible Verse: And thou saidst, I will surely do thee good (Genesis 32:12).

Do you ever need to be reminded of something?

I do. I can be quite forgetful. If it was just left up to me to remember things, I'd never get anything done. In fact, I don't think I would even remember to get up in the morning unless I had an alarm clock. I have a diary where I write things down. I have sticky notes that I put on my fridge door. My phone is full of alarms – one even sounds like a cockerel crowing. I have to be careful to remember to switch that alarm off if I am going to a meeting. Cock-a-doodle-doo is quite distracting to hear when you're in the middle of speaking to someone.

God isn't forgetful – not at all. He doesn't need a diary or an alarm to prompt him to do something. The only thing he forgets is the sins of those who trust in his Son. That's when God chooses to forget our sins because they have been forgiven by him.

However, although God isn't absent-minded, he likes us to remind him of what he has said. So, if we come to God with trusting hearts we can say to him, 'Do you remember, God, what you said you would do?' This is not to refresh God's memory but ours. God's word is given, not for his sake, but for ours. We are the ones that forget about God and his Word. God's Word has been given to us not to help God but to help us.

The more we think about God's promises, and speak to God about them, the more we will be encouraged. We can come to the Creator of the whole universe and say, 'You said this.' God hasn't forgotten he said it, but he wants you to remember what he has said.

There are a great many wonderful promises that God has made, but one of God's promises is, 'I will certainly do you good.' Look at that word 'certainly'. When you read out the verse, say that word extra loudly. It's important. God will do us good, real good, lasting good, only good, every good. He will even make us good – how wonderful. For all those who trust in Jesus there is the promise of eternal life in heaven with him. That is the best ever good that there ever could be.

 What you should do: Remember the promises and 'remind' God of them too, so you will remember them better. God's promises strengthen us and comfort us. Believe that God always does what he has said he will do.

Prayer: Dear Heavenly Father, thank you that you are not forgetful of me. Thank you that, with your power and faithfulness, I can trust you to do everything well. Amen.

9. Words have Meaning

Chequebook Date: 7 June
Bible Verse: And I give unto them eternal life; and they shall never perish, neither shall any man pluck them out of my hand (John 10:28).

Words are important.

We use words to speak to one another and share information. How many words do you think you might know if you counted them? Someone who is three years old probably knows about 300 words. If you are five years old that number has increased to 5,000. By the time you are twelve you will know around 12,000 different words. And each word has its own meaning.

There are a few words that can have several meanings. There are some words that have two totally opposite meanings. Take the word 'fast' for example. It can mean moving quickly, but it can also mean being fixed firmly in place. Thankfully, most words only have one meaning. So, when you hear a word you know exactly what it means.

When we read God's Word it's important to understand what he is saying, and not to make God's Word mean something that suits us. Some people don't like being told what to do. So, when they read God's Word they think, 'God didn't mean that.' But God's Word is true and faithful and there is a verse in the Bible that says we are not to add anything to God's Word or take anything away. It is God's Word and we can rest secure that he means what he says and that what he says is true.

In today's Bible verse, God is telling his people that those who trust in him have a safety that lasts forever. God is saying that he gives his people eternal life. Eternal means forever. It's a life that lasts for all time and beyond. Eternity is something that does not end. So the child of God can be certain that they will live forever. God has promised an eternal life, not a temporary one. When the Lord God speaks of eternal life that definitely shuts out the possibility of any end.

God also says that his people will never perish – which means that they are utterly safe. Their sins have been forgiven. There is no prospect of eternal punishment and they will have a beautiful, sin-free life in their future. That's what those words mean and there is nothing that can change their meaning.

 What you should do: Believe in God's Word and pray to him that you will understand its true meaning.

Prayer: Dear God, and loving Heavenly Father, help me understand your Word, help me to believe in it and cherish it for it is always true. Amen.

10. Hold Tight

Chequebook Date: 7 June
Bible Verse: And I give unto them eternal life;
and they shall never perish, neither shall any man
pluck them out of my hand (John 10:28).

'Hold my hand tightly.'

That's what a parent will say to a young child when they are walking through town. But it's not really the child's grasp that is keeping them safe, it is that of the parent.

When we think about how God keeps his children safe, it is because he is strong and he is faithful. He never forgets his children in an absent-minded way.

There is a verse in the Bible that says that God's children are engraved in the palm of his hand. This means that we must be safe in the grasp of an Almighty Saviour.

44

When I engrave or write something in the palm of my hand, it is because I am by nature quite a forgetful person. I take a pen and write things like: 'Buy milk' or 'Pay that bill' or 'Buy a birthday card.' These words sit there on my hand so that I see them all the time and hopefully attend to the task I need to do. However, if I wash my hands in hot, soapy water, the pen is scrubbed off.

This is not the kind of writing or engraving that God does. These are just some picture words that tell us God will never forget us. We are close to his mind and his heart. God's children are eternally safe.

Why are God's children so safe? It is because they are right in the middle of God's hand. His grip is strong and there is no one who can pluck them out of his grasp.

God's children are eternally secure because they belong to Christ and he will never lose them. The Lord Jesus died instead of sinners. His blood has bought forgiveness and freedom for those who trust in him. When you trust in Christ you are a gift that God the Father has given to God the Son. You belong to him.

Be careful with words, especially the Word of God. Treasure these words and their meaning. Believe them. What God says is the most true and precious word there is. In God's Word, the Bible, there is no error, no unnecessary words, and no missing words. Everything is there that needs to be. Every one of his words is there for a reason.

When we trust in God and his Word, we trust in a good thing. We have no need to fear. But be careful not to be confident in anything else. The only place true rest can be found is when you rest in the hollow of God's hand.

What you should do: Believe in God's Word and trust that he will accomplish it. Do not put your confidence in anything else.

Prayer: Dear God, when I hear your Word help me to respect it for it comes from you. Thank you that I can be certain that every word that comes from you is true. Amen.

11. Enemies Think Twice!

Chequebook Date: 23 June & 29 July
Bible Verses: Therefore thus saith the LORD concerning the king of Assyria. He shall not come into this city, nor shoot an arrow there, nor come before it with shield, nor cast a bank against it (2 Kings 19:32).
He hath cast out thine enemy (Zephaniah 3:15).

Have you ever heard a lion roar?

It's deep and loud and its sound can travel for miles. The lion is a type of animal that we call a carnivore or predator. That means it's a meat- eater and a hunter. In the Bible, David told King Saul about how he stopped a lion in the middle of attacking one of his lambs. The young shepherd boy went after the beast and rescued the lamb from its very jaws. Predators like this were an expected danger in the life of a shepherd in Bible times. They had to be on their guard.

The King of Assyria was like a wild lion to God's people, the Israelites. He was their enemy. King Hezekiah was worried that this vicious ruler would overthrow the land of Israel. Sennacherib, who ruled Assyria, thought he was going to crush the Lord's people, but in the end he didn't even shoot a single arrow. Sennacherib's plans were not God's plans.

People who do not follow the Lord God often cause problems for those who do. God's people often have enemies who are mean to them. Sometimes this is simply mean words. Other times it can be worse. But this only provides God with an opportunity to show how powerful and wise he is. God can physically stop these enemies with his power.

The real enemy of God's people, however, is sin and the devil. Sin can attack us from inside. Our thoughts and desires can turn us away from God, but God's power can turn us back to him.

The devil can also tempt us away from God. He prowls around like a lion seeking to devour those who trust in the Lord. But God can stop him in his tracks too. The evil one tries to trick his way into our thoughts, but God will not allow him to have any real power there. God tells the devil to be quiet so he slinks away and one day God will chuck him out for good!

So, when you feel afraid of death, sin and the devil, trust in God. God can defeat the worst enemies. The devil may fight back – but God's people are perfectly safe from all harm. Even in the middle of death, they can be certain of eternal life because of God's salvation.

What you should do: Trust in the Lord and keep his way, and he will take care of us. He will fill us with wondering praise as we see how he perfectly delivers us.

Prayer: Dear loving Heavenly Father, there is no one who can defeat you. I know that in life and in death you are the winner. Amen.

12. Saying Goodbye

Chequebook Date: 1 July
Bible Verse: God shall be with you
(Genesis 48:21).

The little dog loved his master.

Every time his owner went out the door to go to work or the shops, the dog started to whine. He didn't realise that his owner would eventually come back. The dog was sure he would never see his beloved master again. He thought he was saying goodbye forever. When the master came back, the dog would give him an ecstatic welcome, but the next time he left it was the same. The door would close and the dog would whine.

It can be hard though to say goodbye, can't it? Sometimes, we don't know when or if we will see our friend again. However, if you and your loved one trust in the Lord God, your goodbye won't be forever. There is a heaven, an eternal life for all God's children. Death is not the end of life for those who have trusted in Jesus and had their sins forgiven.

In the Bible we read about a father and son who had to say goodbye. Many years before, they had been cruelly separated. Joseph had been sold into slavery and his father, Jacob, had believed he was dead. It was not until many years later that Jacob was reunited with his son. It must have been hard then when Joseph and Jacob realised that Jacob was dying – and that it was time to say goodbye again. However, Jacob could say with confidence to Joseph, 'God will be with you.' Jacob was not leaving Joseph alone and helpless – God would be his strength and his comfort. This goodbye would not last forever. One day heaven would be their forever home.

When our dearest relations, friends or loved ones go to heaven to be with the Lord, we can be comforted by the thought that the Lord is not departed from us, but lives for us, and with us for ever.

God is on our side, which means we are in the very best company ever. Even if we aren't rich or strong, even if people look down on us – we are with God and he is with us. This means that we are always safe because no one can harm those who are close to God. Those who trust in God are so close to him, it's almost as though they are walking underneath his shadow. And that is such a joyful place to be.

Not only is God with us now, but he will be with us right into the future and forever. He will be with us as individuals, with our families and those that we worship God with. The Lord is with those who are with him. There is no greater happiness than that.

What we should do: Be brave and careful. Be full of joy and hope. God's hope is a certain hope.

Prayer: Dear Heavenly Father, thank you that you are with me – now and forever. I have a great hope for eternity because Jesus took the punishment for my sin. Amen.

13. Unexpected Help

Chequebook Date: 4 July
Bible Verse: Man shall not live by bread alone, but by every word that proceedeth out of the mouth of God (Matthew 4:4).

There are lots of stories of God's unexpected help.

Many people who were poor and in great trouble can tell you that God helped them just at the right time – not a moment too soon, or a moment too late. A man called Hudson Taylor was waiting for his wages, but his boss forgot to give them to him. That night, Hudson gave away his last coin to a family in great need. Now he had no money to pay his rent or buy food. He did not know what he was going to do but hoped that God would help him. The following day, after he had eaten the last bit of porridge from his cupboard, Hudson's landlady came to give him a package that had been left for him at her door. There was no name on it, so Hudson could not work out who had posted it. When Hudson opened the package, inside he found a pair of gloves and a gold coin – enough to pay his rent and buy food. What a relief. That same day, Hudson's boss remembered to pay his wages! So, God provided for all of Hudson's needs and more.

Another man, called George Müller, looked after poor boys and girls who did not have any parents. They all lived together in a big house called an orphanage. Often the children would sit down at the dining table without any food to eat. Just at the last minute someone would arrive with a box full of groceries – enough to feed them all. One day, the building needed to have a lot of work done to it. The heating would have to be turned off even though the weather was very cold. George prayed to God for help and God provided it by changing the weather from being very cold to being lovely and warm. The workers did the work in record time and the children weren't cold one bit.

God provides for us in many different ways. You might think that you get your food from the supermarket; that your parents pay for it out of their wages — and that would be true. But the real person we need to thank for our daily bread is the one who created it in the first place, who waters the fields and who gives us our appetites. However, in today's Bible verse, God is telling us that we need more than just physical food or bread. We could not live for a moment without God's Word. How is that? Well, it was by God's Word that we were created and it is by God's Word alone that we continue to exist. God keeps everything alive by the Word of his power. The Lord God, himself, is the first reason that we are alive.

Hudson Taylor and George Müller were absolutely certain that God was their helper. They saw it with their own eyes. Hudson got a gold coin in the post just at the right time. George had so many mouths to feed, but

God always provided, even when there was nothing in the bank. But both George and Hudson knew that God's Word was what they needed most.

It is with God's Word alone that we can stand up to the devil. If we didn't have God's Word, the enemy would have us in his power. Our souls need food, and there is no better food for them than the Word of the Lord. All the books and all the preachers in the world cannot by themselves satisfy a Christian. It is only the Word from the mouth of God that can do this.

What you should do: Make sure you feed your soul by reading and listening to the Word of God. Pray that God will help you to understand what he says.

Prayer: Heavenly Father, thank you that you feed my body and my soul. You give me my life and existence. You do not need anything or anyone to exist yourself. Forgive me for my sins and give me eternal life. Amen.

14. The Night Sky

Chequebook Date: 6 July
Bible Verse: For God so loved the World, that
he gave his only begotten Son, that whosoever
believeth in him should not perish, but have
everlasting life (John 3:16).

How would you find your way around the ocean?

You don't have buildings or signposts in the middle of the sea. Today there are maps and satellites to help sailors find their way, but in the past, maps weren't always accurate and there wasn't even electricity to light a lamp. In those days, sailors had to find their way by using the stars. The 'pole star' or 'north star' is a very important star for a sailor to use in his navigations. It is the brightest star in the sky and with the right calculations it can show a sailor which way is north because its position is directly above the north pole. All the other stars appear to move slowly from east to west as the earth rotates, but the pole star stays put.

So, if you want to work out how to cross the sea, you need the pole star. If you want to work out how to have your sins forgiven, you need to understand today's Bible verse. John 3:16 is an unmoveable truth that teaches us about salvation.

There are two special words in this verse that shine like brilliant stars. John 3:16 tells us about: Love.

God is love and this verse tells us that God's love is very great. The little word 'so' tells us that God's love is great and measureless.

The second shining word is: Gift.

God gave us something. A free gift – God's Son, Jesus Christ. He is such a unique gift you could never put a price on him. To save us from sin, God sent his Son to die so that those who trust in him can be cleansed from all sin.

The Bible tells us that all have sinned and that God is giving this gift of his love and mercy to 'whosoever believes in him'. The word 'whosoever' is a big word that covers a lot of people. It means that anyone who believes shall not perish, but have everlasting life.

What a great promise – believers in Jesus shall not perish. They are safe in God's love and care.

What you should do: Believers in Jesus shall not perish, but have everlasting life. This is comforting to anyone who is in danger of eternal punishment and cannot save himself. Believe in the Lord Jesus, and you will have eternal life.

Prayer: Dear loving Heavenly Father, I cannot save myself. Only the death of your Son can cleanse me from sin. Thank you that you are able and willing to do that. Amen.

Promises from God for you

And the LORD, He is the One who goes before you. He will be with you, He will not leave you nor forsake you: do not fear nor be dismayed (Deuteronomy 31:8).

These things I have spoken to you, that in Me you may have peace. In the world you will have tribulation: but be of good cheer, I have overcome the world (John 16:33).

I will instruct you and teach you in the way you should go; I will guide you with My eye (Psalm 32:8).

Now the Lord is the Spirit; and where the Spirit of the Lord is, there is liberty (2 Corinthians 3:17).

As for you also, because of the blood of your covenant, I will set your prisoners free from the waterless pit (Zechariah 9:11).

And you shall know the truth, and the truth shall make you free (John 8:32).

15. Family Futures

Chequebook Date: 1 August
Bible Verse: And I will establish my covenant
between me and thee and thy seed after thee in
their generations for an everlasting covenant, to
be a God unto thee, and to thy seed after thee
(Genesis 17:7).

Do you ever wonder about the future, or the past?

Do you try to picture what your grandparents
or great-grandparents were like? Do you
wonder if you will ever have children of your
own? Will they look like you? One of the words
that the Bible uses for the children that
come from a mother and a father is 'seed'.
That is because children are like little seeds.
A seed doesn't stay a seed forever, it grows
and becomes a shoot and then a plant. A child

grows in a similar way. In fact, if an auntie hasn't seen you for a while, when she comes to visit she might say, 'Wow! You've shot up! What's your mum feeding you?'

God has lots of promises for families. His love for his people is so strong that he makes the promise in today's Bible verse to them and to their children, grandchildren and great-grandchildren.

However, just because your mum and dad believe in Jesus, that doesn't mean you are automatically going to heaven. Just because your granny loved God and was forgiven for her sin, that doesn't mean that you directly inherit forgiveness for sin through her. That is not how it works. You need to be sorry and repent of your own sin. You need to come to Jesus Christ yourself. Everyone who ever existed was 'born in sin and shapen in iniquity.' Even before you were born, when you were still inside your mother's womb, you were a sinner. You hadn't stolen anything, or hurt anyone, or even said a bad word, but the desires to do all these things were there in your little heart.

In the end, nobody taught you to lie – you just did it anyway. That's the disease of sin. It is there from your very beginning.

If you haven't trusted in Jesus to forgive you for your sins – that is your first priority. You must turn away from sin to God. Ask him to cleanse you from sin, from its guilt and power and make you his very own child. This is why the Lord Jesus Christ came to this world – to die for the ungodly.

If you have trusted in Jesus to forgive you for your sins – you must pray for others. Pray for your friends and family that they will come to trust in Jesus for themselves. Pray to God that you will marry a godly husband or wife and that both of you will bring up the children that he gives you to trust and honour God. Pray for the next generation that, though they are sinners like you, they will also trust in God as you do.

It is heartbreaking for Christians to see their children and grandchildren turning away from God. However, God hears and answers prayer. So we should pray first for ourselves:

that we will reject sin and accept the gift of salvation from God's loving hands. Then we should pray that God will bless our family and future family. Pray that God's promises will be accepted and treasured by your children and grandchildren and by their children and grandchildren.

What you should do: Remember that without Christ you are a lost sinner. Pray to God for forgiveness. Pray for those you know who have not trusted in Christ. Pray for future generations too.

Prayer: Dear Lord God, I pray for my descendants throughout all generations. Be their God as you are mine. My highest honour is that you have allowed me to serve you; may I and the family that come after me serve you in all years to come. Amen.

16. Light in the Dark

Chequebook Date: 12 August
Bible Verse: For thou art my lamp, O LORD: and
the LORD will lighten my darkness
(2 Samuel 22:29).

Light is so bright.

Even a tiny candle can be seen from far away on a dark night. When there are a lot of lights all shining together, you can hardly see the stars. Sometimes there is so much light that even the birds get a little confused and they call out to each other in the dark.

Towns and cities are now lit by electric light, but it wasn't always like this. A hundred years ago, the streets were lit by gas lamps. Every night, a man was employed to walk the streets to light each lamp along the way. Then, the following morning, he would do the same route in order to turn the gas lamps off. Whether you have gas or electric lights, a big camping torch or a little light from the corner of your phone, they all have the same job to do. They help you see in the dark. Without light you would not be able to find your way along a dark corridor or down a dim alleyway. The light helps you avoid obstacles that would otherwise trip you up.

In today's Bible verse, we are told that God is a light and that without him we are in darkness. This darkness is not the same darkness as night-time darkness. The Bible tells us that we are in a spiritual darkness. Because we are sinners, we are lost and unable to get to heaven, we are not allowed in. Because we are sinners we can't see how much we need God. We need God to show us that we are sinners and that we need him. We need God to forgive us and bring us to heaven, so that we aren't lost forever.

If you have ever been near the coast at night, there is a special light that can sometimes be seen on a cliff top or island. The lighthouse is there to show ships where the dangerous rocks are. The lighthouse can be seen from even twenty miles away.

It is good that we do not have to be close to God in order for him to show us the danger of sin. Even if you have wandered far away from God, he can still reach out and save you.

Sometimes when we are in the dark, we might feel scared. Other times darkness makes us feel depressed. We would rather have a bright sunny day than a dark cloudy one. Spiritual darkness is sad too. If God isn't in our lives, we have no real joy, but as long as God is with us we can have peace even in the middle of suffering. God is like a light that casts a warmth and glow over everything.

Sometimes it can be hard to find joy or happiness. We might go to friends and family to pick us up out of our dark mood, but what if they don't feel happy either? What if the words they say change nothing? What if everything seems so dark that there isn't a single thing in the world that can cheer us or give us joy? Well, there is only one person that we can go to – God. At the very beginning of the world he said, 'Let there be light.' And there was light. He can do the same again.

If you are lost in sin – he can say, 'Let there be light' and he will show you how you need Christ. You will see that trusting in him is the only way that you can be saved.

If you are sad and depressed – he can say, 'Let there be light' and God will give you peace and joy, even though there is still heartache. His words will remind you of his love.

The torch shines in the night, the lighthouse guides the ship safely to shore, God is your light and guide through life.

What you should do: Look to the Lord. When you cannot find a light within you, or your friends, or the whole world, the Lord can speak you into sunshine. You shall not die, but live.

Prayer: Dear God, when I feel dark and lonely, may I turn to you for light and friendship. Amen.

17. Fast and Ready

Chequebook Date: 13 August
Bible Verse: It shall come to pass, that before they call, I will answer; and while they are yet speaking, I will hear (Isaiah 65:24).

If you were to run a race in the Olympics, would you win?

If you had to outrun a cheetah, would you succeed? In a running race, a horse will definitely beat a tortoise, but what if they were doing a lettuce-eating competition? How about a snail or a hamster — which of them would get to the other side of the room first? Maybe neither?

Imagine that you are the fastest person in the world because as soon as the starting pistol is fired, you break through the finishing tape. It is almost as though you have run the race before it started. People would gasp in astonishment if they saw that.

God is fast like that – or faster. He hears our prayers before we even say them and answers us in the same speedy manner! Quick work this! He knows what we need before we even pray it. He can look at us and know what our needs are before we do. So, God goes ahead and arranges the answers to our prayers before the need actually arises. He supplies everything we need and organises it to be supplied at just the right time.

A friend of mine, called Helen, once prayed to God that he would supply her with something she really needed. She was working in a hospital in Africa and a baby girl needed a hot-water bottle. However, who would send a hot-water bottle to the middle of the jungle? And she needed it that afternoon. A few moments later, a parcel was left at her door. Inside were lots of things – including a hot-water bottle. Immediately, she took it to the hospital. God had supplied her need there and then, but what was amazing was that the parcel had actually been posted from the United Kingdom six months before. God had known she would need a hot-water bottle and made sure that it arrived just in time.

God is never late because he knows all that there is to know. There is a special word for that which is 'omniscient'. You can sound it out by saying om-nish-ient. Before we even realised that there was going to be a problem, God's strength arrived. What a prayer-answering God we have!

Now here is another question. What would make your voice sound louder than it is? Can you think of ways to make your voice sound quieter? Are you good at paying attention to instructions, even if they are said quietly or loudly?

Well, God is the universe's best listener. Even though he is in heaven and we are on earth, he can make out every word we say. He makes our prayers travel very quickly. When we pray in a way that pleases God, it is as though we are speaking right into God's ear.

God loves us deeply and is always providing for us, even when we forget to ask him, or forget to thank him for what he has already given us. The God we pray to is a loving and patient God who listens to our requests and always gives us what is best. There's nothing too difficult for God. God doesn't always answer 'yes'. He often says 'no'. He can also say 'wait'. Or he might say, 'I've actually got a better idea.'

What you should do: Pray to God and believe that you will be heard.

Prayer: Dear God and loving Heavenly Father, when I pray help me to pray in faith, believing that I shall be heard, and that I shall be answered. I bring my requests to you believing that I have the answer already. Holy Spirit, help me in this! Amen.

18. Find and Seek

Chequebook Date: 23 August
Bible Verse: I love them that love me; and those
that seek me early shall find me (Proverbs 8:17).

Are you an evening or a morning person?

If you're an evening person, like me, you often get a boost of energy later on in the day. Sometimes an evening person is called an owl because, like the owl, they go about doing things when it's dark. A morning person is often nicknamed a lark because, like larks, they are up bright and early to greet the day.

Being on time or early is important in everyday life. The things that we do first thing in the morning often set us up for the rest of the day. Breakfast, for example, is described as the most important meal. Just as it's important to get things right in the morning, it's important to get things right for our whole life – our spiritual life.

God tells us that we need to be early when trusting in Jesus. It is far better to repent of your sins and trust in Jesus when you are young. We need to seek Jesus early in life. If you go into adult life without Jesus you can commit sins that have serious consequences for your body, mind and relationships. Trusting in Jesus early in life can help you avoid those harmful things. It is never too soon to seek the Lord Jesus. Early seekers make certain finders.

Make sure you seek Jesus with determination. Seek Jesus with eagerness. Jesus Christ must be the most important in your life. Give your whole heart to the business of finding out about him, what he has done for you, what he is doing for you now and how to glorify and honour the Lord in your life. Jesus must be above all things. Jesus first. Nothing else.

When you play hide and seek some people are great at hiding. One of my friends hid in a bath once and it took us ages to find him! Finding Jesus is not like that. He doesn't make himself difficult to find. He's not trying to outwit you. He wants to be found, he wants sinners to be saved. When you set out to really seek Jesus, you can be certain that he will be found. But once you've found him the search continues as you can spend your whole life finding out about him, and learning to love him more and more.

Jesus will be a treasure to you and a close companion for life and eternity.

What you should do: Seek Jesus early in life. Happy are the young who spend the morning of their lives with Jesus.

Prayer: Lord Jesus, may I seek you and find you and may I have such satisfaction and joy from you as I continue to seek and find out more about you throughout my life. Amen.

19. Choices, Changes

Chequebook Date: 31 August
Bible Verse: But the word of the Lord endureth for ever. And this is the word which by the gospel is preached unto you (1 Peter 1:25).

I like a quick walk.

Sometimes I like a long walk. It's good to go out in the fresh air for an hour or so. Recently, I have discovered some new places that I have never seen before. There is a secret wood in the middle of my city. There is a quiet little stream at the bottom of my road. And I've discovered that the walk along the local canal is beautiful.

In springtime, there are lots of wild flowers to smell. One week you discover daisies are in bloom, the next week foxgloves and honeysuckle. As the year goes on, different flowers and plants grow in their season and then fade and die. Nature is always changing.

The Bible tells us that human beings are just like the grass in the field. Everything about us, our possessions, our words, ideas, even our bodies will all pass away. Everyone who begins has an end. However, God's Word never changes. God's good news – the gospel of Jesus Christ – is not like anything else.

So what is this good news? Well, it starts with some bad news. All have sinned and cannot match God's perfect standards. Sin deserves everlasting punishment. And there is nothing that anyone can do to change that.

Human beings cannot save themselves from sin. To be rescued from sin, from its guilt and power, we need to be rescued by God. And this is where the good news part comes in. God has had a plan to save sinners from before the beginning of the world.

God sent his Son to die on the cross in the place of sinners, then he rose from the dead to show God's power over death and the grave.

God's good news not only lasts forever, it lives forever. God's Word is alive because God is alive and he has the power to change minds, hearts and lives. God can turn sinners away from sin to himself. That's powerful!

God's Word doesn't change. It is the same today as it was during Jesus' time, and the time of Moses and Abraham.

Your opinion might alter. Someone's opinion of you might change. The truth of God cannot change because God who spoke it in the first place can never ever change.

What you should do: We have a gospel to rejoice in, a word of the Lord upon which we may lean all our weight. 'For ever' includes life, death, judgment, and eternity. Thank the Lord for his everlasting comfort. Feed on the word today, and all the days of your life.

Prayer: Dear Lord and loving Heavenly Father, may I give glory to you and your Son. May I be nourished by your everlasting Word for the rest of my life. Amen.

For this reason we also thank God without ceasing, because when you received the word of God which you heard from us, you welcomed

it not as the word of men, but as it is in truth, the word of God, which also effectively works in you who believe (1 Thessalonians 2:13).

20. Changes, Choices

Chequebook Date: 3 September

Bible Verse: And ye shall know that I am the LORD, when I have opened your graves, O my people, and brought you up out of your graves (Ezekiel 37:13).

Have you ever wanted to look different?

Some of my older friends deliberately changed their appearance recently. Two guys decided that they weren't going to shave. They thought it would be fun to have a beard for a change. Three months later, both decided to shave the beards off. My mum grew her hair because all the hairdressers were closed, so my niece decided to learn how to cut hair by doing a tutorial on-line. Mum was pleased to get her hair cut for free.

Not everyone needs a razor or scissors to change their appearance. Change might happen to you without you even thinking about it. Perhaps someone hasn't seen you in ages and they exclaim, 'My, how you've grown!'

In the Bible, we read about another change that happens which is much more dramatic than a hair cut, or even a growth spurt. This particular change is not a physical one but a spiritual one and it is something that happened to Charles Spurgeon himself when he was quite a young man.

One winter's day, he was walking past a church building when he noticed that the door was open and a service was taking place inside. He went inside for some warmth.

The usual preacher couldn't make it that January morning, so eventually a thin old man went up into the pulpit to preach. The text was, 'Look unto me, and be ye saved, all the ends of the earth.'

After about ten minutes or so, the old man looked at Charles and fixed his eyes on him as if he knew all his heart and said, 'Young man, you look very miserable and you always will be miserable—miserable in life, and miserable in death—if you don't obey my text, but if you obey now, this moment, you will be saved.' Then, lifting up his hands, he shouted, 'Young man, look to Jesus Christ. Look! Look! Look! You have nothing to do but to look and live.'

Charles was shocked, he wasn't used to being spoken to like this from a pulpit but he said later, 'I saw at once the way of salvation ... when I heard that word, 'Look!'

He realised that the precious blood of Jesus Christ had been shed for him and all he needed to do was look to Christ – just look and he would be saved.

This change from a life of sin to salvation is the greatest change that can ever happen to anyone. It means that you are being brought from spiritual death to spiritual life. And with that comes great light and freedom. The life before forgiveness is dark, the life after forgiveness is glorious. There are difficulties and there is suffering, but the burden of sin is taken away and there is a sure and certain hope of eternal life. Not just an eternal spiritual life, but an eternal physical life as there will come a day when the bodies of all those who trust in Jesus will rise from the grave as Jesus did. The risen bodies of God's people will have no pain or illness – they will be perfect. Perfect bodies and perfect souls. No sin to spoil anything. How wonderful that will be.

God is the only one who could do this as he is the Lord and giver of life. He alone has power over life and death. He is the one who saves from sin and gives eternal life. Charles Spurgeon said that God is 'the living God for he made me live. My soul adores him.'

 What you should do: Praise the Lord God for being glorious and merciful and faithful. Praise him for as long as you live.

Prayer: Lord and loving Heavenly Father, thank you that you have the power to change me. Turn my soul into a lover of you rather than a lover of sin. Amen.

21. Hiding in the Storm

Chequebook Date: 15 September
Bible Verse: And a man shall be as an hiding place
from the wind, and a covert from the tempest
(Isaiah 32:2).

A hurricane is coming.

I heard this on the news. People in America are building up defences around beach homes and seaside communities. They are keeping an eye on the weather forecasts and listening to the news on the radio. Some may need to evacuate to get to safety.

Right now it is very calm outside my home. We don't normally get hurricanes in my country, but there can be bad storms at sea. My friend, who is a fisherman, listens to the forecast on the radio every night. With that information he decides if it is safe to sail or not.

Storms are dangerous and sometimes they can come out of nowhere. Sometimes, however, we know that they are coming and we can make decisions to head for safety.

Just as we need protection from a physical storm, we need shelter from the punishment that we deserve for our sin. Today's Bible verse tells us that there is a man who is a hiding place from the storm. The storm is sin and the Lord Jesus Christ is the shelter.

What a hiding place Jesus is for his people! He takes the full force of the storm that should be unleashed on them. When they run to Jesus for safety, he takes the full brunt of the storm in their place. He shelters those who hide themselves in him. That is the only way sinners can escape the anger of God. God must punish sin, but he has provided a way of escape by trusting in his one and only Son, the Lord Jesus.

There are other storms and troubles that Jesus can help us with. People can attack us and try to harm us. We can suffer from sickness, our bodies grow old. We struggle with all sorts of problems. But when we are in the sheltering care of the Lord, we have the comfort of knowing that he has all the power of life and death. We don't need to fear the future – even the very worst things are all under God's control.

So, don't just stand on your own in the storms of life and eternity. Run to Jesus. You can so easily be protected from the righteous anger of God and the fear of death by sheltering in Jesus Christ. Run to him and be at peace.

When things are going well we might think we have nothing to fear. We feel fit and healthy and there is money coming in. We are doing well at school or sports. We are certain that our future is mapped out and everything is great. But when troubles come, they sweep all that certainty away. The things that we trusted in are knocked out of our lives. Instead we should trust in Jesus because he is never knocked over or blown away by any trouble or storm.

If you are out on a mountain and you see a storm coming, you look for a shelter. You might spot a distant cottage and head there, hoping to be allowed in by the owner to wait out the storm. How glad you are when you sit by the fireside with a cup of tea. The wind and the rain are outside and you are cosy inside. When you trust in Jesus, the storms of life will still come, but you will see them, even experience them, while you have peace in the eternal love and power of Jesus Christ.

What you should do: Take advantage of your hiding place in Jesus. What a hiding-place he has been to his people! He shelters those who hide themselves in him. This is how we escape the anger of God, the anger of men, the cares of this life, and the dread of death.

Prayer: Dear Jesus, how loveable you are. How strong your shelter is. I can have peace because you are with me. Help me to trust in you in all things. Amen.

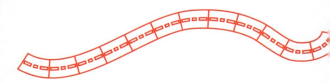

22. God's Music

Chequebook Date: 19 September
Bible Verse: The LORD thy God in the midst of thee is mighty; he will save, he will rejoice over thee with joy; he will rest in his love, he will rejoice over thee with singing (Zephaniah 3:17).

I love music!

One of my first memories is of singing. My mum and dad had an old tape recorder and they recorded me singing a Psalm that they had taught me. When I was scared, I always asked for Psalm 23 to be sung to me. Music can soothe troubles away, it can bring joy. We often find ourselves humming a happy tune or whistling when we are having a lovely day.

It is amazing to think that there is something about God's own children that makes him sing. If you trust in the Lord

Jesus Christ, God is rejoicing over you so much that he breaks into a happy song. What is it about God's children that brings him joy?

Well, we are God's special work. Have you heard the saying, 'Whistle while you work'? If you enjoy your work, it often makes you happy. One of the things that God always enjoys doing is saving. The actual name Jesus means 'the Lord saves'. Saving sinners is something he loves to do. God loves to love. He finds rest in it. Think about something that you love to do after a hard, busy day – something that gives you peace and joy. God's love is what he loves to do. He will never stop loving. And when he looks on you, his beloved, he finds a theme for his song – something that inspires him to sing with great joy.

God has done a great many marvellous things. He has made the world, for example. And when he made the world he didn't sing. He did say, 'It is good.' And when he made human beings he said, 'It is very good.' But he didn't sing. That is something that he kept for his most precious work – saving sinners.

Ever since Adam and Eve chose to sin against God, every human being has done the same thing – sinned. But the Lord God offers salvation to sinners without cost. It is a free gift from him. How wonderful that such a precious gift is given without charge, for we could never earn it. It is too great a treasure to be bought. It is beyond price. Yet, giving this free gift to sinners brings God such joy that he sings.

What you should do: Do not fear any danger for God is mighty to save. There is so much treasure and strength in our God. He is so close to us. Those who trust in him should shout and sing for joy.

Prayer: Loving Lord Jesus, your love is immeasurable. Teach me to love you and rejoice in you. May my life be like a song of joy for you. Amen.

O Lord, hear! O Lord, forgive! O Lord, listen and act! (Daniel 9:19).

Charles Spurgeon
Who Is the Greatest?
Catherine MacKenzie

Charles Spurgeon preached from the Bible in a way that ordinary people could understand. He even acted out Bible passages and would pace back and forth dramatically! He was a great preacher, but he knew that it was God who was behind this. It was God who made Spurgeon great.

ISBN: 978-1-5271-0393-1

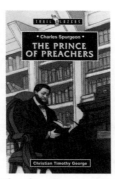

Charles Spurgeon
Prince of Preachers
Christian George

Charles Spurgeon was a simple country lad who went on to become one of the best known preachers in London, Europe and the world. Caught in a snowstorm one day when he was a teenager, he crept into the back of a church and the words, "Look unto Jesus and be saved!" changed his whole life. Charles spoke words that touched the hearts of rich and poor alike. His fame became so widespread that it is reputed that even Queen Victoria went to hear one of his sermons. Charles was more concerned about the King of Kings – Jesus Christ.

ISBN: 978-1-78191-528-8

Christian Focus Publications publishes books for adults and children under its four main imprints: Christian Focus, CF4K, Mentor and Christian Heritage. Our books reflect our conviction that God's Word is reliable and Jesus is the way to know him, and live for ever with him.

Our children's publication list includes a Sunday School curriculum that covers pre-school to early teens, and puzzle and activity books. We also publish personal and family devotional titles, biographies and inspirational stories that children will love.

If you are looking for quality Bible teaching for children then we have an excellent range of Bible stories and age-specific theological books.

From pre-school board books to teenage apologetics, we have it covered!

Find us at our web page:
www.christianfocus.com